FOR

GLORIA & GWEN,

MOTHERS WHO UPLIFT SO MANY.

—A.D.P. & B.P.

CONTENTS

MARTIN RISING

BY Andrea Davis Pinkney

REQUIEM
FOR A
KING

PAINTINGS BY **Brian Pinkney**

SCHOLASTIC PRESS / NEW YORK

Library of Congress Cataloging-in-Publication Data

Names: Pinkney, Andrea Davis, author. | Pinkney, J. Brian, illustrator.

Title: Martin rising : requiem for a King / by Andrea Davis Pinkney ; paintings by Brian Pinkney.

Description: New York : Scholastic Press, [2018] | Includes bibliographical references.

Identifiers: LCCN 2016031408 | ISBN 9780545702539 (hardcover : acid-free paper)

Subjects: LCSH: King, Martin Luther, Jr. 1929-1968–Poetry.

Classification: LCC PS3616.I574 A6 2017 | DDC 811/.6–dc23

LC record available at https://lccn.loc.gov/2016031408

10 9 8 7 6 5 4 3 2 1   18 19 20 21 22

Printed in China 38   First edition, January 2018

Excerpts from Martin Luther King, Jr.'s "Mountaintop" speech were reprinted by arrangement with The

Heirs to the Estate of Martin Luther King, Jr., c/o Writers House as agent for the proprietor New York, NY.

Copyright © 1968 Dr. Martin Luther King, Jr. © Renewed 1996 Coretta Scott King.

Photos ©: 118 top: Donald Uhrbrock/The LIFE Images Collection/Getty Images;

119 top: Jack Thornell/AP Images; 119 center: Bettmann/Getty Images;

119 bottom: Bettmann/Getty Images; 120 top: Shelby County Register's Office/Archives;

120 center: *Washington Post*/Getty Images; 120 bottom: AFP/Getty Images;

121 top left: Bettmann/Getty Images; 121 bottom: © Bob Adelman.

DAWN

HENNY PENNY PRELUDE

Here she is!

Hind feathers
hightailing.

Her birdie eyes,
filled with foresight,
see far down the road.

Peck-peck prophecy.

Henny Penny.
Know-it-all she-bird.

Guards her eggs
like a mystery-riddle.

Invites us to inquire:

What's inside the future's shell?
Who holds the yolk of tomorrow?
When the time comes,
what cracks open?
Can chicks survive after the sky falls?

DAYLIGHT

SPARKLING-EYED CHILD

JANUARY 15, 1929

Baby boy born,
eyes sparkling.
Martin.

Came into this "Jim Crow" world
brought daylight to
this unfair world,
this legal-to-cheat blacks world,
with God-given gifts:

big voice,
sharp mind,
sparkling-eyed vision
that could see something special
in tomorrow's promise.

He studied
oratory,
sociology,
theology,
and excelled.

When he became
a full-grown man,
he found a place in history
as he fulfilled his destiny to
fight for full equality:

as scholar,
preacher,
believer,
and teacher of what it means to dream.

With those sparkling eyes always looking ahead,
Martin found the path
of light, of love, and truth,
the Bible, his beacon.

He stepped right up to the teachings
that nourished the world's greatest minds:

Lincoln,
Thoreau,
Tolstoy—
and Gandhi, (whose heart was warmed
by the wisdom woven
in the Sermon on the Mount.)

These greats were Martin's North Star.
The compass
that led him to the mountaintop.
He knew, deep down, he had to climb
to reach the promised land—
along with his close companion:

Nonviolence.

And so,
Martin took that trip.

Rode
   the Montgomery bus boycott.
Strode
   through Selma.
Wrote
   a letter from Birmingham Jail.
Marched
   on Washington
where he told his eager followers:
"*I have a dream!*"

On that unforgettable day—
glorious,
triumphant—
on that peace-filled afternoon,
when not one drop of violence spilled,
what did the now-a-man,
who was once
the gifted child with sparkling eyes,
see into Future's face?

Did he know what Horizon's hand held?

Did he understand that to be born
with so many gifts
was a privilege that had a price?

How *could* he know?
How *could* he foretell?

To come so far,
to stand so high,
all he knew
was that he had to keep climbing
                    to the top
                         of the mountain
                              at all costs.

It seems that Martin
the sparkling-eyed child born
leader of his people
was put here to do
just that.

HAPPY BIRTHDAY, DADDY!

JANUARY 15, 1968

Thirty-nine candles
on a buttercream cake!

A sweet birthday mix
of sugar and vanilla.

A cinnamon pinch
invites good luck.

Batter drips
thick ribbons
on this just-right gift.

Two tin pans
slide from the oven
in a Georgia kitchen.

Golden moons,
sweet steam rising,
cooled,
stacked,
ready to be dressed
in snowy-colored
cloaks
for the birthday party
of a lifetime.

Whipped egg whites
form frothy frosting,
licked clean
from Coretta's wooden spoon.

Eager fingers scoop
the spoon's delight.

 Yolanda,
   Martin III,
    Dexter,
     Bernice.

Martin's children
chant:

Happy Birthday, Dear Daddy!

17

Laughter.
Tickles.

Make a wish!

One steady heave
of his barrel chest.

Puffed cheeks,
then—quick!—
a mighty *blowwww . . .*

Out go
the tiny flares,
sending itty-bitty smoke stacks
into a cloud that surrounds
Martin's Papa Bear grin.

The candle-smoke haze
forms a halo of happy
round this family fun.

Coretta corrals
her brood,
gathers them
while she plays
proud piano.

Butterscotch fingers
grace eighty-eight
keys
that unlock
celebration songs
for Daddy!

Spirituals,
R & B,
silly ditties
fill the room.

Fill these hearts
with so much love.

Papa Bear Martin
hugs his cubs.

Somebody shouts,
Let's all sing!

A King chorus
rejoices:

This little light of mine . . .

Shoo-be-doo-be-doo-da-day . . .

Merrily,

merrily,

merrily,

life is but a dream . . .

FORCING FORSYTHIA

FEBRUARY 11, 1968

Impatient for winter's end,
gardeners trudge through
snow-crusted beds
smothered in stubborn white,
refusing to melt from fence posts and lawns.

The most determined search for ready bushes
crisscrossed with jutting branches.

Twisted, eager candidates
shooting forth
to greet sharpened pruning shears.
Clip-snap! Snip! Snip!

Gathered twiglets,
stems soaked
in warm water.

Wet promise
that will course through twiglet veins.

Coaxing, cajoling, forcing
forsythia's
frilly flowers.

So golden.
So pretty.

Proud,
smiling from a cold steamed window
frozen shut against winter's final weeks.

20

In Memphis, Tennessee,
on this same frigid February day,
another kind of flower rears *its* face.
Twisted, ugly blooms
of discrimination.

On this day in the heart of Tennessee,
a.k.a. the Volunteer State,
branches of the city's government
refuse black sanitation workers equal pay.

These garbage collectors
have not volunteered for *this*.

They have not raised their hands
for degradation.

Yet, like forsythia, they are forced.

Forced
to slog through snowy streets,
gathering rotted trash and waste.

Forced
to take low wages.

Forced
to drive broken trucks.

Forced
to work when sick.

Forced
to collect paychecks
that can't afford coats for their
children, who shiver and are hungry
on this day
in Tennessee—the Volunteer State.

Ten days ago,
when two garbage collectors,
seeking shelter from heavy rains
in their truck's compactor,
are crushed,
all the sanitation workers are
forced
to speak up.

Their pleas are ignored.

Their requests silenced.

Their civil rights neglected.

Their humanity rejected.

Enough! they shout.
Enough!

These mistreated workers
are forced
to strike.

For unlike
forsythia's budding twiglets,

forced men,

eager for equality,

do not blossom.

VALENTINE

FEBRUARY 14, 1968

Martin once said:
*"We must meet the forces of hate
with the power of Love."*

Martin once said:
*"I have decided to stick with love.
Hate is too great a burden to bear."*

Martin once said:
*"Love is the key to the solution
of the problems of the world."*

Martin once said:
"Love your enemies."

On this day
of doily hearts,
and gold-foil candy,
and the Supremes' "Baby Love" wishes,
folks in Memphis
are down on their knees
proposing to Equality:

Be mine!

COME

Oh *come*, all ye faithful!

Ministers by the hundreds
form a group
to support the sanitation strikers.

They meet in a church basement
dank with mold,
brimming with hope.

Come,
say the clergymen to the strikers.

Pray with us.

Stay
as close as you can
to the Lord's handiwork.

That night,
among church basement
votives
and the smell of vestry mothballs,
those who have come
are blessed with
G-O-D—the Gift of Desperation.

Out from this extreme
they create
a way to galvanize.

Come,
they cry
to townsfolk, to families,
to congregants,
to kids.

Come.

That is when the Lord's handiwork
starts to stitch itself
into the fabric of their intention.

Come.

Through the Gift of Desperation
comes the name of their striker's group:

Community on the Move for Equality—COME!

COME—committed
to nonviolence.

COME—civil disobedience
with not a trace of hatred.

COME—unity to meet Memphis head-on
in loving protest.

But, Lord,
even with your handiwork
hard at work,
it is *hard, hard* work
not to strike back violently,
especially when you're striking.

But, O Lord, thank goodness
for COME's leader:

The Reverend James Lawson,
a disciple and good friend
of Dr. Martin Luther King, Jr.,
a founder
of the Student Nonviolent Coordinating Committee,
knower
of what it takes to proceed
with silent serenity.

Lawson—who holds close
to Dr. King's Dream.

Lawson,
like King,
deeply
devoted to peace.

EARLY SIGNS
OF SPRING

Henny Penny would have squawked, but good.

The sky is falling!
But had that feathery chick
been darting through the segregated soils
of Memphis on that thundery day,
she would have known better.

Though spring was coming,
though major-league
pitchers and catchers
were ready to play,

Though fast, black-cleated runners
rounded second base,
carrying out Jackie Robinson's
well-crossed color line,
the clouds above Henny's head
hadn't spilled a bag of baseballs.

Oh, no, no.

That thundering tarnation
was the weatherman's prediction,
pushing through colorless airwaves
on Tennessee's radio station WDIA.

For once, in the Deep South's
Confederate blue moon,
the weatherman's prediction was coming true—
storm warning in effect.

Oh no!
So much weather worry.

Too much dread
as spring unfurls.

Henny Penny,
awaiting Easter eggs,
emerald grass,
jelly beans.

Darn this blasted
gloom-doom sky.

Squawk!

Oh no!

Had Henny not been pecking seed
or yanking worms
from Memphis dirt,
she could have warned us all
of what would soon
come falling.

Squawk!

ROAR!

MARCH 11, 1968

In like a lion,
the month of changing seasons
charges ahead.

Blustery squalls
filled with flurries
threaten us with winter's
bleak,
bleached
sky.

Groundhog,
where are you?

Get back up out that hole!

Poke your nose
with a proud twitch
toward the
pale,
unripened peach meat
that is our month-of-March sun.

Groundhog, no!
It can't be true!
Are you sure you saw your shadow
back in February?

More wintery weeks
in Memphis, Tennessee?

Groundhog, what is that dark expression
forming in your eyes?

33

I know that look.
I've owned that look.

It's oppression,
humiliation,
pure and simple.

No matter what
your whiskers
have revealed,
March poses no threat to
the sanitation strikers
who march through March
in Memphis.

Schoolkids join the strikers' march,
black and white,
together
they protest quietly, peacefully
under Reverend Lawson's leadership.

They cling
to the peace-dream
of Dr. Martin Luther King, Jr.

Yes, they march through March
alongside garbagemen
who hold up their heads,
gaze straight,
never losing sight of the filth
that piles high as they strike.

But their efforts pack
little power.
They're disorganized.

On a big hill called Memphis
they appear as itty-bitty ants,
needing more leadership,
trying to fight the grizzly bear of injustice.

Skitter-scatter,
crawling
among the rubble of their refusal
to work
in such dirt.

Refusing the refuse on the dirty streets
            slick with blackened banana peels,

    rotted squash,

        eggshell junk,

    mustard stains.

Remnants
these strikers
will not collect.

More than one hundred of us—
kids, ministers, sanitation workers—
are thrown in jail.

Quietly, peacefully, the marchers go.

Incarcerated for their intention.

Imprisoned for marching through March.

Not only do they refuse to collect
filth from the Memphis streets
in the Volunteer State,
they will not succumb to
violence.

These strikers have volunteered for
peaceful protest.

When the police handcuff
and shove them,
and choke hold their hope,
and cart them away,
these men and women,
and girls and boys
who have volunteered
for self-dignity,
will not
enter jail
in the same way
March
enters the calendar.

These strong, quiet
strikers,
and all who stand by them,
refuse to Roar.

Going out like lambs,
they are ignored.

No better pay.
No benefits.
No fair working conditions.

No progress.

WEATHER NEWS, BASEBALL BLUES

MARCH 17, 1968

On WDIA radio
the weatherman
socks it straight.

A forecast
not meant for weary souls
or fainthearted baseball fans:

Wind,

thunder,

lightning striking.

A curveball faster
than a pitch on opening day,
when hundreds
pour themselves into stadium seats
to watch the Memphis Blues play.

White fans park in down-close seats
near the dugout.

Black fans
must sit

    high

  high

far away from home base
on benches in
the nosebleed section
where the altitude
is *steep*.

Where they're closer to WDIA's
weather news.

But boo to you, WDIA!

Ain't no black folks

    up

  up

  today in nosebleed seats.

Let the wind blow!
Let thunder roll!
Lightning, go 'head—strike!
'Cause we're striking, too (but losing faith).

Got our name in the paper, though:
Community on the Move for Equality
C-O-M-E
Marching men, growing weak.
Strikers losing steam.

Three days ago,
through a crackly phone line
Reverend James Lawson placed an important call.

Urgent
with the Gift of Desperation.

Imploring COME.

Come,
please come.

The strikers need you.
Memphis needs you.

Friend, I need you.

Martin, come.

Announcement today:
MARTIN IS COMING!

KINGS IN MEMPHIS

MARCH 18, 1968

Martin arrives
in Memphis.

He's *come* to help
his friend.

He's *come* to
inspire.

To bring a bit of sun to
this rainy town,
where another King—Elvis himself—
reigns over his Graceland estate.

A mansion with a swimming pool and jukebox,
oblivious to the plight
of workers,
marchers,
strikers,
whose struggle to feed and clothe their kids
drags across town
from the black-iron gates
of Elvis's opulent place.

Forged in music, those gates keep the
rock-and-roll King
cloistered from the
conflict just miles away.

When Martin,
the King of *his* people,
arrives,
he delivers words
that are eloquent
and packed with the grace
of a thousand Gracelands.

At Mason Temple Church of God in Christ,
to the largest indoor gathering
in the fight for civil rights,
Martin delivers a gift—
the flip side of desperation.

Fifteen thousand listeners,
blessed to hear
Martin bestow a new offering:

"*The time is now*," he says.

These word-gifts,
spoken
in the fourteenth
of more than thirty speeches
Martin would give this week,
in many US states of desperation,
in cities and churches,
and backwater towns
that dot
Southern soil,
imploring their King:

Please COME.

To conclude the word-gifts
that buoyed his people on this
still-winter night,
Martin places a bright bow of hope on top.

He promises to return
in four days—March 22—
to lead a large,
organized protest
through Memphis streets,
beyond Graceland's gates,
piercing any remaining ignorance
that persists in this Volunteer State.

SMOTHERED

MARCH 22, 1968

Thunder!

      Lightning!

Workers
      striking!

Then,
sudden spring flurries.

Then,

Snow
      Snow
Snow

In Memphis
and everyplace else that calls Tennessee home,
weather-related regret.

The blizzard blanket
smothers
Martin's ability to
come.
      Hope dashed!

        Martin's trip
        canceled.

SHATTERED

MARCH 28, 1968

Out
like a lamb.

March, you are fickle,
unpredictable,
tricky.

Today is hot.

Sticky.

The peach-meat
sun
is an ochre ball.

Beating its heat,

down,

     down,

drowning winter,
inviting forsythia
to gladden gardens
with its own natural blooming
rhythm.

It's a good thing, too.

Those frilly flowers are welcome bouquets
for Martin's return
to Memphis.

The sanitation workers' march starts.

Eleven o'clock,
on the nose
of what they hope
will be
freedom's punctuality.

Garbagemen go all out.

All showing up,
so proud.

Boys and girls—twenty-two thousand of them!—

Playing hooky, skipping school,
so they, too,
can demonstrate.

Martin leads them all
through Memphis streets
toward city hall.

Arm in arm,
he walks,
with his friend,
his ace,
his close-close confidant,
Reverend Ralph Abernathy.

Interlocked elbows,
the city's many ministers
march with Martin, too.

We shall overcome!

Their anthem is punctuated
with signs carried front and center
by striking workers
who are still invisible
to the prejudiced eyes
of city officials.

Four words
shout simple affirmations
of their humanity:

I <u>AM</u> A MAN

<u>I</u> AM A MAN

I AM A <u>MAN</u>

These banners incite.

They rile.

They inflame so much anger
in the strikers' hearts.

<u>*I AM A MAN*</u>

Four words
churn the innards of the men,
who today,
under the peach-meat
ochre sun,
clearly see
the nonentities
they have become
in the minds of many.

In Memphis, Tennessee.

The peaceful march
goes quickly south.

Takes a turn
of the worst kind—
violence!

Fathers,
brothers,
black mothers' sons.

Humiliated by their
second-class status,
sick of striking,
strike out.

Hurling glass bottles
against the pavement, painted hot by ripened peach-meat.

Smashing windows
to loot what they could never
afford on their lower-than-the-curb
paychecks.

Breaking into local stores.
Taking revenge.
Snatching back lifetimes of stolen entitlement!

An eye for an eye. A tooth for a tooth.
We are all blind and toothless now.

Their rage explodes into a full-scale riot.

Police!

    Billy clubs!

Tear gas!

    Crying.

Gasping.

Prayers for fresh air . . . suffocated.

March over,
Martin declares.

The King's resolve is shattered
into heartsick shards.

To Ralph,
his close-close ace,
his right-hand man,
Martin utters doubt
in his Dream
for peace.

Martin confides in his friend
that he's afraid to hear the voice of violence,
a flashing siren,
approaching.

STILL STANDING

MARCH 29, 1968

Dozens of guardsmen
with bayonets
have been beckoned
to keep
at bay
the remaining
diehards
who are hard-pressed
to lay down
the last-gasp
signs
of their dignity.

Still they march,
footsore,
strong-willed:

I AM A MAN.

SKY TRUTH

APRIL 1, 1968

Call this a day for Fools.

For tricks, pranks,
unexpected games.

For lies even.

Chumps, beware!
Keep your eyes wide open.

See what's in front of you.

Don't ignore
deceits
right beneath
your nose.

Around the corner,
a wise guy waits
to put a tack on your chair,
a plastic roach in your sheets,
wads of Wrigley's in your hair.

But gullible one,
take comfort in
your own instinct.

Go with your gut.

If your insides tell you *no*,
then *don't* go.

If you're uncertain,
look to the sky.

She will never lie to you.

Her open sheet,
her cape of many colors,
always speaks the truth.

The sky's eyes
are always wide.

Even on April's first day,
Lady Sky is no fool.

Martin looks to her for guidance.

A sign—any direction at all.

What of Memphis?

His friends say stay home.
Colleagues urge—*Let it be.*

        But Lady Sky—Mama Fate—she has other plans.

A clear message comes to Martin:

*March again
in Memphis.*

Give peace its chance.

BRAVURA BIRD

Henny Penny,
tired backside.

She's been warming those baby eggs
for what seems like ten forevers.

And *whew*,
those little globes have grown.

Their speckled shells
are hard against Henny Penny's pillowy nest.

They press
at Henny's hiney feathers,
worn from keeping them warm
for so many days and nights.

But soon, oh, soon,
their beaks will poke.

They'll fight their way
into this world with every bit of chick-grit
their tiny, slimy baby muscles can muster.

What will they find when they arrive?

This question,
not a mystery-riddle
to Henny Penny.

Prophetic bird coos:

*Mine eyes have seen
what's beyond
my eggs' fragility.*

DARKNESS

FOREBODING

APRIL 3, 1968 ~ RUNWAY DELAY

WDIA—not again!
Please!
No more weary weather news!

Memphis
deluged
under the blows of a thunderstorm.

And there goes Henny Penny.

Squawking 'bout something falling down.

Her hurly-burly foreboding
means nothing to Martin.

His mind is made up.
He is scheduled to speak tonight.

And days later,
he will lead another march,
sure to bring strikers
their due.

Determined,
Martin dozes on a Memphis-bound plane,
waiting for takeoff.

On the runway,
seat belt tight,
he wakes with a start.

Sweaty,
running a fever.

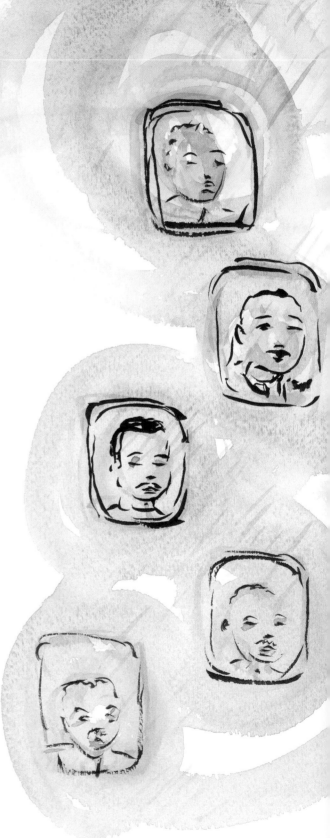

At the same time,
shrugging off a chill
that clings
to his clammy suit and tie.

The King travels with friends
who insisted
on coming along for the ride.

Fellow reverends,
all close:

Ralph Abernathy,
Jesse Jackson,
Bernard Lee,
Andrew Young.

The plane
will not budge.

They are waiting, waiting,
waiting.

Finally, the captain's drawl
comes through sputters on a speaker.

From the cockpit,
his twang is filled with fake assurance.

A bomb scare, he announces.
But all clear now . . . No reason to fret . . . Friendly skies.

That captain—what an actor.
Sunny talk while a threat looms.

Cold comfort as the welded eagle
lifts its iron tail
off the runway,
forging its silver nose
toward more Memphis rain.

HOME AWAY FROM HOME

APRIL 3, 1968 ~ EVENING AT THE LORRAINE MOTEL

Thank goodness
for the Lorraine Motel,
in the heart of black Memphis.

Home away from home.
Warm comfort for Martin and his roommate, Ralph.
Room 306–$13.00 a night.

Fresh sheets.

Clean towels.

Packaged soaps:
waxy, tiny, fragrant.
Like the forsythia, now blooming full.

But Martin, he is wilting.

The bomb scare has made him weary.
His fever hangs on like a weighty wool coat, two sizes too small.

This worn-thin minister
needs to save his energy for the march on April 8.

Martin asks his ace to deliver tonight's speech,
to show up
at the Mason Temple rally in his stead.

Ralph agrees.

FEVER

APRIL 3, 1968 ~ SAME EVENING AT THE MOTEL

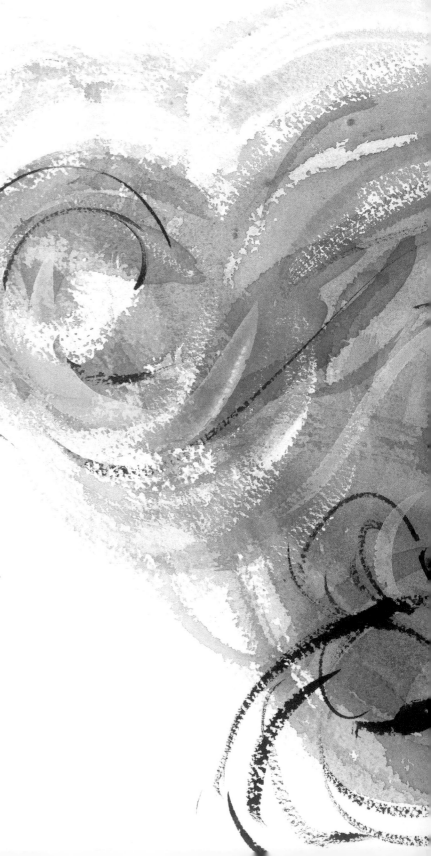

Even a King can succumb
to a fever's pitch.

Overtaken by
delirium's dizzying dreams,
Martin can't seem to shake
the heat
that rises
from a place deep within him.

He wishes he could
beg off,
stay in bed,
skip the speech.
Just this once.

But that'll never do.
Especially when Ralph
calls him at the Lorraine.

Martin, they want you.
They want your words.
Your wisdom.

Your wings
that can fly against
the tide of rain covering Memphis
in a thick sheet
of painfully slow progress.

Martin trembles,
shrugs,

Wills himself
to show up for a
                    steep,
              steep,

climb

to the Mountaintop
of premonition.

Goaded by his own knowing,
forgetting his umbrella,
legs heavy,
Martin ventures out,
on this hammer-rain night,
soaked,
his fever raging.

Mason Temple, here he comes.

To deliver
his final torrent.

STORM

APRIL 3, 1968 ~ NIGHT AT THE MASON TEMPLE

The sky.

Sickly green swirls
lace its black cape.

Can the elements get any more ugly?

Hard to believe,
but, yes, it's true.

On this hammer-rain night
Radio station WDIA has upped the ante:

Strong winds,
a hissing locomotive.

Tornado watch!

Forsythia branches,
torn from pretty bushes.
Whirligigs batting at the wind.

Martin rushes in
through the side door of Mason Temple,
sudden as the thunderclap
smacking the back
of his tight-seamed suit.

Good Lord—a horde welcomes this mighty minister,
still wearily under the weather,
but renewed of spirit
when he sees thousands of smiles
greet his arrival.

His lectern awaits.

A hush swells.

Martin blots his brow.

Pauses.

Prays silently.

Speaks.

HEAVEN'S RAILROAD

APRIL 3, 1968 ~ MARTIN'S SPEECH BEGINS

First comes the flight.

The Almighty has granted
Martin a bird's-eye journey,
an escape from here and now.

With his listeners riding
in the palms of his hands,
Martin guides them.

To Egypt's Red Sea,
Greece,
Rome,
the Renaissance.

Behold the majesty
of history's lessons.

"*But I wouldn't stop there!*" he declares.

Martin's words pull us forward
on this passage through time.

With King as conductor
on heaven's railroad,
high above the ground,
we roll ahead.

To Mr. Lincoln's
urgent Emancipation.

To FDR's
"*Nothing to fear but fear itself.*"

History's trip holds the roadmap to progress,
Martin proclaims.

"But I wouldn't stop there!"

His words,
coursing wind,
fill the wings
that lift this crowd,
enraptured.

Martin talks of
trouble in the land.

Confusion all around.

But he lifts them with
his wisdom:

*"Only when it is
dark enough
can you see the stars,"* he says.

Tonight,
Martin is the star,
the North Star,
the beacon-leader who lights the way.

With all who have gathered,
now fully following Martin's
words,
this bird's-eye trip
lands
where I <u>AM</u> A MAN first took *its* flight—Memphis.

Martin implores us to
stay the course.

To move through the ugliness that
has been heaped
onto Memphis workers,
wanting justice:

      Peace,
      peace,
      only peace.

His message is simple,
and the same as it has been since the beginning
of every journey:

*"It is no longer a choice
between violence and nonviolence
in this world."*

Nonviolence or nonexistence—that's the choice.

That's our ticket
to freedom's destination.

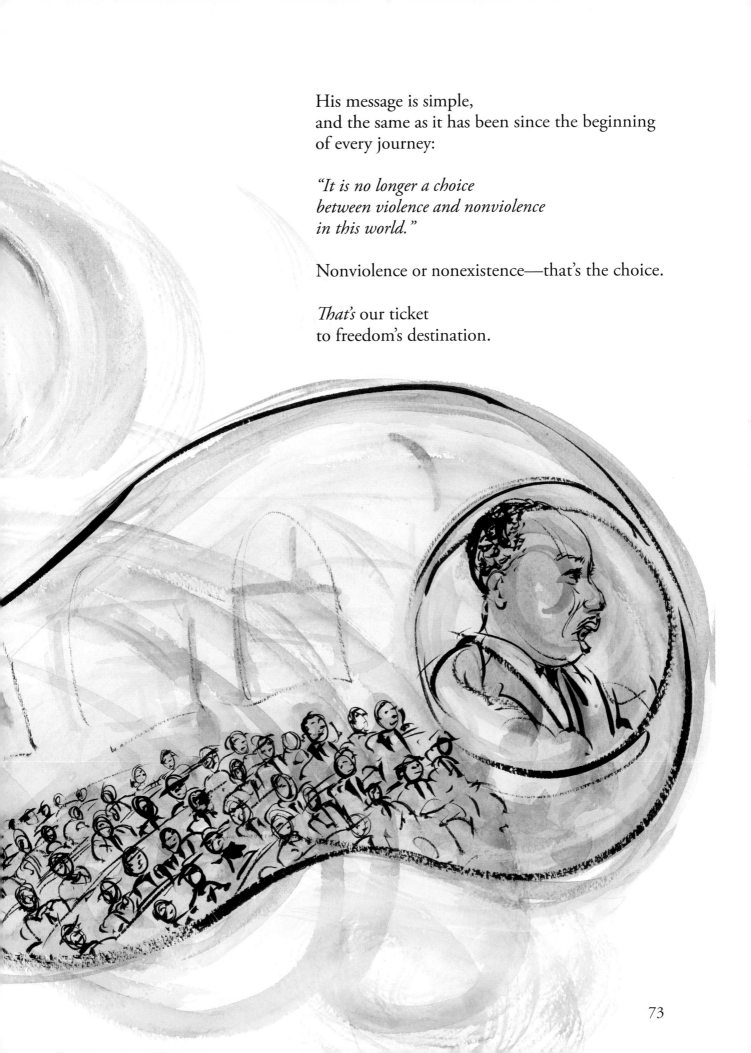

MINE EYES HAVE SEEN

HIS SPEECH CONTINUES ~ IT ROLLS, LIFTS, PREDICTS

Now,
the vision.

The soul's knowing.

Foreshadow.

Martin calls us to action:

"Rise up tonight with a greater readiness!"

But are we truly ready for what's to come?

Outside,
the hammer-down rain
is an iron fist.

Good Lord, this rain!

Will it ever quit?

Relentless,
spitting with a will,
it stings.

Good Lord, this rain!
Slinging pings of premonition.

Though Mason Temple is dry inside,
Martin is drenched,
sweating.

Fever.

As he speaks,
his gaze lifts to a far-off place.

Martin,
he sees something
in the gray-gloom sky.

Senses doom
on that
blurred horizon.

The knowing soul in Martin's eye
sees far
into the rain outside.

   Foreboding.

But still,
Martin's words
roll ahead with a thunder
that only *he* can bring.

He tells of the airplane bomb scare.

He speaks of threats,
and his view from high up.

This seeing man's words overtake him.

They push,
blurt into the edge-of-their-seats crowd.

Martin tells it like it is—and like it will be:

"I would like to live a long life.
      Longevity has its place.
      But I'm not concerned about that now.
      I just want to do God's will."

Every edge-of-their-seat
I <u>AM</u> A MAN,
every dressed-in-her-best woman,
every sanitation striker,
and rain-slicked baby,
who has come with Martin

through tonight's journey,
honors him with cheers of praise.

The heated crowd
fuels Martin's fever-pitch delivery,
now spiked high.

And,
in a sudden revelation,
Martin Luther King, Jr.
delivers his own deliverance.

Here,
tonight,
fueled by his Godly vision
Martin has climbed to the highest mountain peak.

"And I've looked over,
        and I've seen the promised land.

"I may not get there with you.

"But I want you to know tonight,
        that we,
        as a people,
        will get to the promised land!"

The rain slams down,
ruthless,
alive.

Bone-deep inside himself,
Martin's Henny Penny premonitions
know what the sky will do.

Brow-to-brow with that monster
called Mortality,
he holds fast to his faith.

"I'm not fearing any man.
        Mine eyes have seen the glory of the coming of the Lord!"

SLEEP

APRIL 3, 1968 ~ LATE NIGHT

After battering southern Tennessee
with its punches,
Heavyweight Rain,
who has pummeled the pulp out of Memphis,
finally sleeps.

Heavyweight Rain has left thick air
and the smell of wet streets
in its wake.

All kinds of rain has a way of doing that—lingering,
sometimes beautifully,
sometimes hauntingly.

Tonight,
Rain's reminder hangs on
with dark, damp hands.

Back at the Lorraine Motel,
Martin stays up most of the night
with his friends,
joking, laughing,
giddy after his speech.

DAY BREAKS

APRIL 4, 1968

When dawn starts to climb,
Martin, like the rain, dozes.

Thank goodness for the quiet
of Room 306.

Thank goodness for the Lorraine Motel,
his home away from home.

Thank goodness for a roommate like Ralph,
who keeps Martin's spirits up
and his schedule straight.

Tonight,
another rally.

Tonight,
another gathering
of workers,
and wives,
and babies bundled tight.

Tonight,
a new journey.

But for now,
as his fever wanes,
Martin sleeps,
and sleeps,
and *sleeps*,
till noon.

Till Ralph nudges,
prods,
wakes his friend,
who is true-deep dreaming.

Ralph is ready to roll.

There is planning to do
for a second march in four days,
in support of the garbage collectors.

A second stand
for I <u>AM</u> A MAN.

This time,
we pray,
it will be a march of
     peace,
     peace,
     only peace.

PILLOW FIGHT!

APRIL 4, 1968 ~ LATE AFTERNOON

Martin is still weary,
so weary.

And discouraged
by the strike's slow progress.

Truth is,
even after his journey on heaven's railroad
took him to a giddy place,
even though his eyes have seen a pretty mountain peak,
King is downright depressed.

His brother, Alfred Daniel,
nicknamed A.D.,
has come to Memphis
to surprise him.

Good friends and a good brother
are strong medicine
when you're bone-tired and feeling low.

Everybody gathers in A.D.'s motel room, where they bring
a big dose of playtime.

They jostle Martin, shake off his weariness.

Martin may be tired, but, man, you can't lead
a movement when Papa Blues has got his iron arms tight around you.

King shakes off that blue papa by taking the first swing—
a floppy feather pillow at Andrew Young.

Andrew comes back fast,
lands a slap—*bam!*—
onto Martin's head.

He clobbers King!

Then Ralph and A.D.
join the puff-slaps.

Game *on*—grown men, pillow fightin'!

Belly-good laughter for longtime buddies.

Giggling,
like tomorrow is never gonna come.

Cracking up,
like the weary ways of yesterday are gone.

Now is the time for all-good.

Brother-friends,
having fun!

With so much pillow slammin' and carrying on,
these brother-friends have worked up
grown-men appetites.

SOUL FIXIN'S

APRIL 4, 1968 ~ EARLY EVENING

Thankfully, suppertime's coming.

Almost six o'clock.

Time to get ready.

No doubt folks began lining up at
Mason Temple's front door as soon as the sun
started to dip its chin into the Memphis hills.

Back in Room 306,
Martin and Ralph dress quickly.

White shirts,
pressed
crisp as the sky.

Heavyweight Rain has taken a break.

Martin and Ralph each wear
a necktie.

Each knotted with a steady hand,
as only a gentleman can.

Before tonight's rally,
a meal is planned at the home of Reverend Billy Kyles
whose wife, Gwen, is,
right this minute, in the Kyles' kitchen
stirring up what's good for hardworking, pillow-fightin' men.
She's fixing to serve on the front lines of equality's battle.

Gwen has made fixin's for the soul:
roast beef, candied yams, turnip greens.

God bless, Sister Gwen.

And Martin can hardly wait
to leave the Lorraine, and head to the Kyles' home to eat.
He can practically smell that roast
splitting open its sure-is-good promise.

    Soul fixin's, here comes Martin.

Outside,
the sky is a clear opal cape,
wearing a halo made by the sun

      setting,

      slowly,

      slowly.

QUICK-STRANGE!

APRIL 4, 1968 ~ NIGHT APPROACHES

Dressed as the man of distinction that he is,
Martin steps out onto the balcony
of his home away from home.

Onto the fresh-air terrace of the Lorraine Motel,
breathing in the evening.
Sun's burnt-pearl has painted the sky.

So lovely, so calming.

Twilight's hush welcomes Martin with

    stillness.

From inside Room 306, Ralph hears it first.

A dull,
sudden . . .

    Pop!

Quick-strange wonderings flood Ralph's mind:

    What on earth?

    A cranky car?

    A firecracker?

Ralph rushes to see.

    Lord, have mercy!

POWERLESS

TIME-OUT OF TIME

Brave bird,
wings blurred
in a flutter-flap frenzy.

She tries, oh, she tries
to fly
in the bullet's face

Tries to dance in front
of its path.

Tries, oh, she tries.
So hard
she tries.

This determined bird
works her wings
with the might of a mama
protecting her young
from oncoming harm.

Brings it on
in a frenzied dance.

Tries to stop Time.
Works double time to distract Death.
Maybe her flapping can divert its path.

In full-out center-stage fashion,
she extends both wings,
chest wide open.

A feathery cross,
that bird.

A brave shield of showy,
flappy feathers.

Hoping to block
the unstoppable
oncoming train-of-pain locomotive
speeding toward
sparkling-eyed Martin.

But no matter how hard
she works her wings—
no matter how much she
tries to deflect
the inevitable—

nothing can erase the name
etched in the bullet's face.

Powerless bird,
forced to surrender,
is the first to cry.

COMPASS

Martin!

His white shirt—spattered red!

His necktie tie,
ripped off
by the force of that anonymous *pop!*

The tie's black-and-gold stripes
have been flung
every which way.

The necktie's tail—flipped, crooked, cockamamie—
is a needle pointing north
on a compass whose every arrow
leads to peace.

Martin Luther King, Jr.

Hungry for that sure-is-good food for the soul,
his last supper, ripped away like a broken promise.
The repast waits, losing its sweet steam,
while Gwen wonders, *What's keeping Martin?*

He's laid out flat
on the home-away-from-home welcome mat,
whose name is Lorraine.

Brother. Friend. King.

No!
It can't be!

That once baby boy,
sparkling-eyed child.

Believer.
        Dream weaver.
Papa Bear—mighty *blowww*.

Come, all ye faithful.
All aboard heaven's railroad!

The Higher Side's torch rests by the open door,
inviting him to fly.

            COME home.
            Time for supper, child.

And so I'm happy tonight.

            No!

I am not fearing . . .

Know God, know peace.

            No! Stop! Can't be!

Mine eyes have seen the Glory . . .

Good-bye, brother-friends . . .

Good-bye, Lorraine . . .

    I <u>AM</u> A MAN

Spiritual food
for weary souls—slain!

PRONOUNCEMENT

APRIL 4, 1968 ~ 7:05 PM

Radio WDIA
socks it straight.

This is not a forecast.

It is official:

> *Martin Luther King, Jr.*
>
> *Thirty-nine years old.*
>
> *No longer a flesh-and-blood man.*
>
> *Now a martyr of mercy.*
>
> *Now above the rain.*
>
> *Past the clouds.*
>
> *Beyond*
> *each*
> *and every*
> *thunderstorm.*

Henny Penny tucks her beak
under her beaten wing.

Speckle-feathered mourning bird
who cannot flutter free
of her own sad prediction
come true.

> The sky has fallen.

CHAOS

APRIL 5 AND 6, 1968

Heaven help us,
Please, Dear Lord.

The sky's on fire!
The sky's torn loose!

Burned off its hinges!

Smacked down—*thwak!*

Can't run for cover
when the whole sky
comes crashing,
crushing,
bearing hard,
pressing the breath
from our lungs.

Flying ash—that sky.

Burned everything
out their sockets—
eyes,
innards,
toenails even.

That bearing-hard sky.
It's shocked us all!

Snatched the skin
right off our flesh.

Gouged the gristle
clean from our bones.

Feels like hell's here,
searing.

Hurts worse than hell, that fallen sky.

Is this some kind of repentance for our people?
Is there an unknown crime,
greedy
to collect its pay?

What did we ever do to deserve this?

What did *he* ever do?

With Martin gone,
we're broken,
raging,
looting,
screaming.

      Baseball bats!

    Angry fists alight with fire!
              Smashing glass!
       Disbelieving.
   Confused.
        Choking on smoke.
     What side's up?
    What side's down?

   Hell's come to earth.

  The sky's the ground!

BABY JAMES

Did his mother cradle
her newborn boy?

Did her infant wriggle
as she counted ten piggy toes?

Was he pink,
peaked,
jaundiced?

Did his tiny soul,
once clean,
know it would someday
be soiled by hate?

Does a future killer coo
when his baby cheeks get kissed?

So many questions
whose answers remain
hidden by the Dark Angel
who,
like a petty thief,
snatched James Earl Ray's innocence.

Lured him,
from the time he was
old enough to read,
down a crooked path:

Kid bully.

Criminal.

Mail fraud.

Armed robberies.

Prison escapes.

Mug shots
where wild eyes
pierced their sockets.

Repeat offender.
Until,
one day,
Baby James,
all grown up,
becomes what
every mother fears.

A troubled son,
turned assassin.

Pleading guilty.

Sentenced to ninety-nine years.

UNSOLVED HISTORY

He's the terrorist in our textbooks,

the classroom subject
of conspiracy theories.

Who was Martin's true assassin?

Like the scratch on a forty-five,
the needle gets stuck,
grooved in one spot that repeats the same question.

Motive?
Motive?
Motive?

And speaking of a scratch,
history has forever scratched its head
on this.

Some are 100 percent sure it was Ray.
Others say, *No, keep investigating.*

And so, it remains an unsolved history.

Can we ever set the record straight?

Class, it's time for a test.
Please fill in the blanks.

1. Did somebody put him up to it?

2. Who sent that mother's-son-gone-wrong
   on an evil errand?

3. Was that troubled one a villain,
   or the victim of
   some perverse pressure?

4. Who told him, *Go fetch a Remington rifle*?

5. People said he was "the alleged." The so-called.
   True or False?

6. Is the government the guilty party?

Pencils down, students.
Time's up on this unsolved history test.

These are not trick questions,
and there are no sure answers.

DESPERATE QUESTIONS

RECITATIVE FOR ALL DAYS

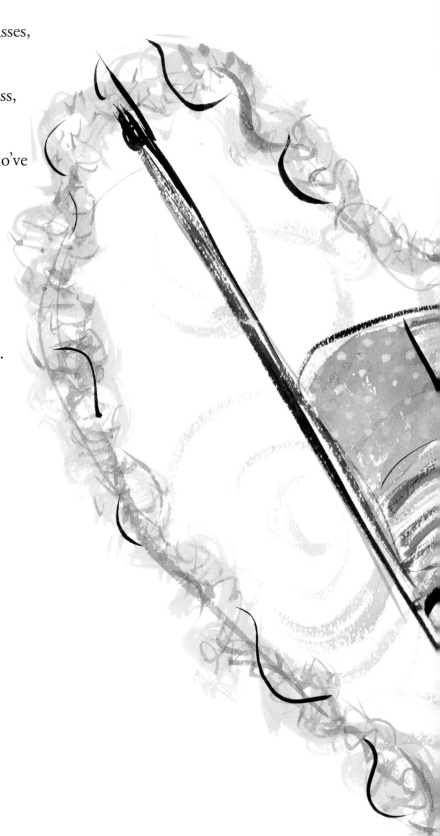

When your wife or husband passes,
they call you a widow.

When your mama and papa pass,
you're an orphan.

But what will they name us who've
lost our shining-light leader?

Yes, we've lost him.
So, call us that.
Lost.

In the forest,
blinking into darkness,
calling out for our missing one.
Henny asks:

Martin, where are you?

LAMENTATION

APRIL 7, 1968

Half-mast flags
wilt in somber winds,
limp from the loss of
our leader.

Stars and stripes,
aimlessly dangling,
are ashamed to be
symbols of a country
that claims it is
the land of the free.

In yards and fields,
on flagpoles and fence posts,
our star-spangled banner
is a small patch
in a soul-searing story
that has now spread far beyond Memphis.

On this Day of Mourning,
in every state of grief,
the Promised Land is broken.

The whole world weeps.

QUIET STORM

APRIL 8, 1968

Coretta
carries herself with a black swan's dignity.

Glides through Memphis streets
on feet
determined to move
her husband's legacy ahead.

A mourner's march,
a striker's procession,
rolled into one powerful
peace-river
overflowing its banks.

Out front, eyes intent,
here she comes.

Coretta Scott King,
and her children.

Tennessee strikers
follow behind.

See the swell
of thousands.
Witness the multitudes.
Ponder the mystery.

So many marchers,
who make not a sound,
coursing the road to Jericho.

Coretta's quiet storm,
her silent thunder,
pushes past
all ignorance.

Peace marchers
hold fast in their minds
to the words they once carried on signs:

I AM A MAN

I AM A MAN

I AM A MAN

Coretta's grace
inspires striding,
ignites silent pride.

Coretta Scott King
marches for Martin,
no longer at her side.

DADDY

APRIL 9, 1968 ~ MORNING MOURNING

Four flowers,
so beautiful.

Their blooming stunted
by sudden grief.

Yolanda,
  Martin III,
    Dexter,
      Bernice.

These little ones,
the sun glints
in young Martin's eyes.

Struggling now
to make sense
of sudden lightning.

Daddy,
snatched,
plucked,
stolen—in a blink!–
by the hand of a man
filled with hate.

Four flowers,
sweet-pea children
at the center of Martin's Dream.

He and Coretta's
brown-sugar blessings.

Their reason
for following the dove's refrain.

Peace,
peace,
only peace.

And Mahalia Jackson sang
one of Martin's favorites:

"Take my hand, precious Lord."

Choruses of comfort,
prayer-songs,
hoping that every child-flower,
everywhere,
will someday be free
to gladden its garden.

Yolanda,
  Martin III,
    Dexter,
      Bernice.

Faces buried in their mother's
skirt,

tear-soaked.

105

PILGRIMAGE

APRIL 9, 1968 ~ AFTER-MOURNING MORNING

Atlanta streets,
a bottlenecked swarm
of footsore souls,
unfurl in a funeral procession.

Sad steps paint the wailing veil.

Lost moths
whose dust-powdered wings
flit in a frantic parade,
eager to draw warmth
from the rickety mule-drawn hearse
that carries their resting King.

DAWN

GOOD FRIDAY

APRIL 12, 1968

Sorrow,
settled like fog,
has a golden roof
that can only be seen
from above its shingles.

Looking down from atop Sorrow's canopy,
gray-opaque
is dappled with warmth.

Peach-meat,
finally ripened,
spills brilliance.

    Sorrow, you are a stubborn cloud that clings.
    But did you see sunset's hidden promise?

There is hope in the gloaming!

EASTER SUNDAY

APRIL 14, 1968

Children rise as morning dawns,
greeting the sky,
a rolled-out piecrust.

Out they go,
dressed in ribbons, bowties,
patent-leather toes,
knees greased.

Ready for church,
eager to receive a sunrise sermon.

This is the day the Lord hath made!
Let us rejoice!

So much golden hope
on the horizon.

So much *light*.

Yes,
here it comes!

Sun!
Sun!

Stretching between hillcrests,
dappled, winking.

Martin's memory
shines as bright
as daffodils,
tulips,
orchids,
blooming in so many hearts.

Gladness fills every pocket
of every giggle
that is shared by boys and girls
of every complexion.

And look,
over there,
on the velvet-grass hill.

Henny Penny,
bonnet cocked,
bumbling behind her—*surprise!*—
downy baby sweetie pies.

Hope abounds
before our eyes.

REJOICE THE LEGACY

JANUARY 15 ~ MARTIN LUTHER KING DAY ~ FOREVER

Peck-peck proclamation:
when the sky falls,
it can also rise.

And so, today, though his candles stopped
at thirty-nine,
we celebrate Martin's exquisite life.

His sparkling-eyed vision
of tomorrow's promise.
His destiny.
His dream.

How he led us to the mountaintop
on the path of light, love, and truth.
He didn't get there with us.
But he showed us the way.

So today we stand together.
We remember.
We recite.
We, who believe,
rejoice his legacy.
A national holiday for MLK!

And yet, we still cry
for that darkest hour
for his soul's middle passage
through ugly seas.

But in the swill of our tears, we find gladness, too.
Because, from the blackness of unknowing,
a sliver of light shines through trees of grief,
illuminating the answer to an urgent question:

Can a Dream ever die?

A burst of sun replies:

His life well lived for peace and good.

Martin's spirit—still alive!

And with love,

we all shall rise.

AUTHOR'S REFLECTIONS

These poems tell a true story of a cherished leader's final days. And they speak of a time when African Americans faced an uncertain future. But at the moment of their greatest hope, the sky seemed to be cracking at its very core. Freedom and equality for some in this country were as fragile as eggshells. How was change ever to come?

In preparing to create this narrative, I searched my heart for what I've come to look for as "the way in." How, I wondered, would I be able to deliver Martin's heartbreaking story? Soon, the portal that opens up to reveal its lighted path to a story shone brightly. This would be a requiem to honor Martin, and to illuminate the hope that rises out of darkness.

Written in a narrative form that I call "docu-poems," these vignettes highlight the events as they unfolded during the days and weeks leading up to Martin's death. And they also seek to honor the lives and spirits of the sanitation workers who worked closely with Martin and who believed in and followed his dreams. It is my hope that each poem brings insight and dignity to the men and women who risked everything to end injustice, while also painting the story of humanity's power, against all odds, to change the world by working peacefully together.

The narratives can be read silently or performed publicly. Group readings aloud will let readers experience history in the making as well as its emotional depths. Wonderful classroom plays of *Martin Rising* can be performed by using the "Now Is the Time" history on pages 118-121 as narration — and adding selected poems from the book to tell the story!

At the same time, it is my hope that *Martin Rising* can serve as a compelling journey through history that allows readers to discover their own "way in" to a past time and place. And that it will inspire them with events that still positively impact our lives today.

A word about Henny Penny. She's the one who started all of this by presenting herself to me in a dream.

Some will ask: *Who is this being?*

Henny Penny is the omniscient existence of wisdom, an elder presence that illuminates, punctuates, foretells. She is the Greek chorus in this play. She is a protector, a mother bird, a knower. You can call her a squall, a cloud, loud tidings, a truth-teacher, a preacher, a church lady. For me, Henny Penny is like the sky's ever-present insight. She is the essence of eternal expectation. But please interpret her as you wish. She is whatever spirit-power you need her to be.

—ANDREA DAVIS PINKNEY

ARTIST'S REFLECTIONS

When I began working on the images for *Martin Rising*, I was flooded with emotion from both the soaring spiritual heights of Martin's life, as well as the tragic and violent end of one of my greatest heroes. I was also elevated by the power and spirit of the protesters who lifted Martin and the movement to their greatest impact. I wanted to convey all this through my renderings—but without literally showing all the actual events. Instead, I sought to illuminate the spiritual implications by expressing what history books don't often fully convey—the metaphorical.

But how would I do this? I began by seeking inspiration from artists like Marc Chagall, and also the African American artist Norman Lewis, who worked during the civil rights movement and rendered history through abstract expressionism rather than through literal depictions. I then created visual metaphors to symbolize how Martin embraced his own family with his love—a love that started in Martin's own heart, was shared in his home, and ultimately cast its luminescent power throughout the world. Repeating symbols of home, family, church, and weather are shown through form, color, and movement. And in my mind's eye, images of Martin rising above the marchers as he rallies them, leads them, and embraces them are what ultimately guided my hand as I created the art for this book.

—BRIAN PINKNEY

NOW IS THE TIME

The plight of the African American people dates back to 1619, when slavery, the ugly institution of human bondage, was brought to our shores. Though slavery had been abolished sixty-three years before Martin was born, its poisonous remnants lingered. In the South, "Jim Crow" segregation laws made the oppression and degradation of black people legal. They were not free to eat, go to school, or take public transportation alongside white people. Adding to this, the right to vote or run for office was routinely obstructed. That deprived them of their rights to elect lawmakers or leaders.

And even after the Civil Rights Act of 1964 and the Voting Rights Act of 1965 were enacted, it still took years to unravel the system of inequality. Martin devoted his life to changing this. And his work continued all the way to these last months of his life—and beyond . . .

Martin Luther King, Jr. was a Baptist minister. He was also a loving father and husband who enjoyed precious time spent with his family.

For thirteen years, Martin inspired millions of people to change America. He was best known for his role in the advancement of civil rights by using nonviolent civil disobedience based on his deep spiritual beliefs.

LIKE MANY OF AMERICA'S WORKING POOR, Memphis sanitation workers endured terrible conditions. They had to pick up stinking, rotting garbage, for which they earned half the salary of their white counterparts. Sometimes their trucks had flat tires or faulty parts. But unlike white workers, if they stayed home during a snowstorm or when they were sick, they could expect less money in their paychecks, or not to be paid at all. On February 1,1968, two sanitation workers, Echol Cole and Robert Walker, were crushed to death in the compactor of a malfunctioning truck.

Within ten days, a two-month strike was set in motion.

Marches, protests, and constant union battles were waged. Soon Martin, who was fighting for equality for the poor, was called in to help organize and act as inspirational speaker and spiritual leader. This strike soon gained national prominence.

On March 18, Martin came to Memphis, where about 15,000 people attended the rally. He promised to return for a citywide march on March 22. But a heavy snowstorm prevented this.

When Martin finally returned to Memphis on March 28, he and Ralph Abernathy (right) led the strikers in a march that was meant to be peaceful, but became violent soon after it started.

Silently, the march continued the next day. Memphis sanitation workers covered the city's streets with their simple, powerful declaration, "I AM A MAN." A new march date was set. Martin planned to be back.

Martin returned to Memphis on April 3. He stayed in the Lorraine Motel—one of the few motels in town that was open to black guests.

That night at the Mason Temple he gave one of the most powerful speeches of his lifetime, "I've Been to the Mountaintop," where he predicted his own death. He had seen the mountaintop, he told the people— but he may not get there with them. And he implored them not to give up the fight.

The following day, Martin was assassinated at the motel. The assassin was James Earl Ray, a prison escapee, drifter, and lifelong criminal. His heinous crime seemed to have no apparent motive.

In the days immediately following Martin's assassination, angry people expressed their feelings of powerlessness over the sudden loss. In 110 American cities, including Washington, DC, Chicago, and Baltimore, as well as in small towns, riots broke out.

On April 8, Martin's wife led the march of Memphis sanitation workers that her husband had come to Memphis to attend. It was a completely silent march that also served as a tribute to Martin. There were 42,000 people participating. Coretta was accompanied by three of their four children, (from left) Yolanda, Martin III, and Dexter, as well as Martin's friends Ralph Abernathy and Andrew Young. How many wondered how much more Martin might have done had he lived? And where would they go from here?

The family and the country were bereft. More than 60,000 people heard the first service for Martin at the Ebenezer Baptist Church outside over loudspeakers. And about 50,000 joined the four-mile procession afterward through downtown Atlanta to Morehouse College for a second service. Many of them sang "We Shall Overcome." Martin's simple casket pulled by a mule-drawn farm cart stood as a symbol for his support for the rights of the poor.

Though Martin did not live to see the conclusion of the strike, his commitment to making lives better brought results. The strike ended on April 16 when negotiators finally reached a deal—allowing the City Council to recognize the union and guarantee a better wage. Today, as we reflect on Martin's legacy, we can embrace his call to action, which remains ever relevant.

When we vote, we rise. When we march, we rise. When we speak out, seek peace, teach the truth, we all rise to a better tomorrow. And the time is now!

121

TIME LINE

HIGHLIGHTS IN THE LIFE AND TIMES OF DR. MARTIN LUTHER KING, JR.

1929 ~ **JANUARY 15:** Born in Atlanta, Georgia, to Alberta Williams King and Martin Luther King, Sr.

1944 ~ **SEPTEMBER 20:** Began his freshman year in the historical Morehouse College at age fifteen.

1946 ~ **AUGUST 6:** Atlanta's largest newspaper, the *Atlantic Constitution*, publishes a powerful letter to the editor about racial equality.

1948 ~ **FEBRUARY 25:** Becomes assistant pastor at Ebenezer Baptist Church in Atlanta.
~ **JUNE 8:** Receives bachelor of arts degree in sociology from Morehouse College.

1951 ~ **MAY 6–8:** Graduates from Crozer with a bachelor of divinity degree; delivers the valedictorian commencement speech.
~ **SEPTEMBER 13:** Begins as a graduate student in systematic theology at Boston University.

1953 ~ **JUNE 18:** Marries Coretta Scott. Later they have four children: Yolanda Denise, Martin Luther III, Dexter Scott, and Bernice Albertine.

1954 ~ **SEPTEMBER 1:** Begins serving as pastor at Dexter Avenue Baptist Church in Montgomery, Alabama.

1955 ~ **JUNE 5:** Receives his doctorate in systematic theology from Boston University.
~ **DECEMBER 5:** Elected president of the newly formed Montgomery Improvement Association (MIA). The MIA facilitates the Montgomery bus boycott.

1957 ~ **JANUARY 10–11:** Appointed chair of the Southern Negro Leaders Conference on Transportation and Nonviolent Integration (later called Southern Christian Leadership Conference, SCLC).
~ **FEBRUARY 18:** Appears on the cover of *Time* magazine for the first time.
~ **MARCH 6:** Meets with Prime Minister Kwame Nkruah at Ghana's indepndnece ceremony in West Africa.
~ **MAY 17:** Delivers his first national address, "Give Us the Ballot," at the Prayer Pilgrimage for Freedom in Washington, DC.
~ **JUNE 13:** Meets with Vice President Richard M. Nixon, requesting that Nixon work on passing the civil rights bill.

1958 ~ **JUNE 23:** Gathers other civil rights leaders to meet with President Dwight D. Eisenhower in Washington, DC, to discuss desegregation in schools and the continuing violence against African Americans.
~ **SEPTEMBER 17:** *Stride Toward Freedom: The Montgomery Story*, his memoir, is released.

1959 ~ **FEBRUARY:** Begins five-week tour of India, and meets with Prime Minister Jawaharlal Nehru.

1960 ~ **FEBRUARY 1:** Moves back to Atlanta from Montgomery to prioritize the SCLC and the struggle for freedom.

1961 ~ **MAY 21:** Addresses a large rally at a Montgomery church after a group of Freedom Riders are attacked for protesting segregated bus terminals.

~ **OCTOBER 16:** Meets with President John F. Kennedy, pressing him to issue a second Emancipation Proclamation to end racial segregation.

1963 ~ **APRIL 16:** Writes the famous "Letter from Birmingham Jail" from a prison cell. The letter justifies the nonviolence tactics for the civil rights movement.

~ **JUNE 5:** *Strength to Love*, a book of sermons, is published.

~ **AUGUST 28:** Delivers "I Have a Dream" speech during the March on Washington, DC, to a crowd of more than 200,000 people.

~ **SEPTEMBER 18:** Gives the eulogy at the funerals of three of the four children murdered during a bombing that occurred three days before at the 16th Street Baptist Church in Birmingham, Alabama.

1964 ~ **JANUARY 3:** Appears on the cover of *Time* magazine as "Man of the Year," the first African American to receive this title.

~ **MARCH 26:** Meets in Washington, DC, with Malcolm X for the first and only time.

~ **JUNE:** *Why We Can't Wait*, his third book, is published.

~ **JUNE 11:** Jailed for demanding service at a "Whites Only" restaurant in St. Augustine, Florida.

~ **JULY 20:** Works with SCLC and CORE (Congress of Racial Equality) to launch People-to-People tour of Mississippi in the Mississippi Freedom Summer campaign.

~ **DECEMBER 10:** Awarded the Nobel Peace Prize at a ceremony in Oslo, Norway. At age thirty-five, King becomes the youngest man, and the second African American, to receive the honor.

1965 ~ **MARCH 21–25:** Successfully leads marchers from Selma to Montgomery, accompanied by civil rights leaders James Forman and John Lewis.

~ **AUGUST 12:** Expresses his opposition to the Vietnam War during a mass rally at the Ninth Annual SCLC Convention in Birmingham.

1966 ~ **FEBRUARY 23:** Meets Nation of Islam leader Elijah Muhammad in Chicago.

~ **JUNE 7:** Continues James Meredith's "March Against Fear" from Memphis, Tennessee, to Jackson, Mississippi, after the attempted assassination of Meredith near Memphis.

1967 ~ **APRIL 4:** Delivers his "Beyond Vietnam" speech in New York City, criticizing the government for investing millions in the Vietnam War, but not putting any money toward blacks who need protection in Selma.

~ **JUNE:** *Where Do We Go from Here: Chaos or Community* is published.

~ **DECEMBER 4:** Publicly announces the Poor People's Campaign in Washington, DC.

1968 ~ TIME LINE FOR MARTIN RISING

~ **FEBRUARY 1:** Two sanitation workers in Memphis, Tennessee, Echol Cole and Robert Walker, are crushed to death in an accident on a city truck.

~ **FEBRUARY 11:** Over 700 men attend a union meeting and unanimously decide to strike the next day.

~ **FEBRUARY 14:** The mayor delivers a back-to-work ultimatum for the following day. Newspapers say more than 10,000 tons of garbage has piled up.

~ **FEBRUARY 24:** After police use mace and tear gas against nonviolent demonstrators, black leaders and ministers meet in a church basement and form Community on the Move for Equality (COME) to support the strike and the boycott.

~ **MARCH 11:** Students skip high school to participate in a march led by black ministers.

~ **MARCH 14:** Ministers implore Martin to come to Memphis.

~ **MARCH 17:** Public announcement is made that Martin is coming.

~ **MARCH 18:** About 15,000 people from Memphis attend a rally. There, Martin calls for a citywide march on March 22. He promises to return.

~ **MARCH 22:** Record snowstorm prevents Martin from returning to Memphis. The march is canceled.

~ **MARCH 28:** Back in Memphis, Martin leads a march from Clayborn Temple that is halted when windows are broken by angry protesters, and police use nightsticks, mace, tear gas, and gunfire to contain the crowd. Many arrests and injuries, and the death of a sixteen-year-old boy. A curfew is authorized and 4,000 National Guardsmen move in.

~ **MARCH 29:** Some 300 sanitation workers and ministers march peacefully and silently, escorted by dozens of Guardsmen with bayonets.

~ **APRIL 3:** Martin comes back to Memphis, where he delivers his "I've Been to the Mountaintop" address.

~ **APRIL 4:** An assassin takes Martin's life as Martin stands on the balcony of his room at the Lorraine Motel.

~ **APRIL 7:** A national day of mourning is proclaimed by President Johnson for this day.

~ **APRIL 8:** To honor her husband, and to support the strikers, Coretta Scott King leads a peaceful silent march through Memphis.

~ **APRIL 9:** Funeral services are held for Martin in Atlanta.

~ **APRIL 16:** Union leaders and city officials reach an agreement, putting an end to the strike.

SOURCES

THE FOLLOWING SOURCES WERE CONSULTED IN THE CREATION OF THIS BOOK.

BOOKS

Adelman, Bob, and Charles Johnson. *Mine Eyes Have Seen: Bearing Witness to the Struggle for Civil Rights.* New York: Thames & Hudson, 2007.

Altman, Susan. *Extraordinary African-Americans: From Colonial to Contemporary Time.* New York: Children's Press, 2001.

Bolden, Tonya. *M.L.K.: Journey of a King.* New York: Abrams Books for Young Readers, 2007.

Branch, Taylor. *The King Years: Historic Moments in the Civil Rights Movement.* New York: Simon & Schuster, 2013. (abridged version of the three volume trilogy)

Carson, Clayborne, and Kris Shepard, eds. *A Call to Conscience: The Landmark Speeches of Dr. Martin Luther King Jr.* New York: Hachette Book Group, 2001.

Carson, Clayborne, David J. Garrow, Gerald Gill, Vincent Harding, and Darlene Clark Hine, eds. *The Eyes on the Prize Civil Rights Reader: Documents, Speeches, and Firsthand Accounts from the Black Freedom Struggle.* New York: Penguin Books, 1991.

Else, Jon, *True South: Henry Hampton and Eyes on the Prize, the Landmark Television Series that Reframed the Civil Rights Movement.* New York: Viking, 2017. Book to accompany PBS Video, *Eyes on the Prize: American's Civil Rights Movement*, Blackside, 2006. (seven-part DVD series).

Jakoubek, Robert. *Martin Luther King, Jr.: Civil Rights Leader.* New York: Chelsea House Publishers, 1989.

Katz, William Loren. *Eyewitness: The Negro in American History (A Living Documentary of the African-American Contribution to American History).* New York: Touchstone, 1995.

King, Martin Luther, Jr. *I Have a Dream.* With foreword by Coretta Scott King. New York: Scholastic Press, 1997.

Johnson, Charles, and Bob Adelman. King: *The Photobiography of Martin Luther King, Jr.* New York: Viking Studio, 2000.

WEB SOURCES

Alverson, M. (2016, April). "Jacquelyn Hawkins, C'71, Remembers Dr. Martin Luther King Jr." Retrieved June 13, 2016, from Spelman University, News and Events, http://www.spelman.edu/about-us/news-and-events/our-stories/stories/2016/04/05/jacquelyn-hawkins

Blumenfeld, W. J. (2016, February 2). "Dr. Martin Luther King Jr.'s 'Inescapable Network of Mutuality.'" *The Huffington Post.* Retrieved from http://www.huffingtonpost.com/warren-j-blumenfeld/mlk-gay-rights_b_1202671.html

Dycus, K. (2014, January 24). "Sharing Dreams: Reflecting on King, Gandhi, and Jainism at Houston's Rothko Chapel." *The Huffington Post.* Retrieved from http://www.huffingtonpost.com/jaina/sharing-dreams-reflecting_b_4593065.html

Estevez, M. (2016, January 19). "Lin-Manuel Miranda as Dr. Martin Luther King, Jr. Is Nothing Short of Amazing." *Vibe.* Retrieved from http://www.vibe.com/2016/01/lin-manuel-miranda-dr-martin-luther-king-speech-nothing-short-of-amazing/

Jones, D. M. (2011, August 22). "Set Yourself Free: The Weight of Hate Is Too Big A Burden." *The Huffington Post*. Retrieved from http://www.huffingtonpost.com/dennis-merritt-jones/fear-into-hate_b_930965.html

Kakutani, M. (2013, August 27). "The Lasting Power of Dr. King's Dream Speech." *The New York Times*. Retrieved from http://www.nytimes.com/2013/08/28/us/the-lasting-power-of-dr-kings-dream-speech.html

King, M. L. (1957, November 17). "Loving Your Enemies" speech. Retrieved June 9, 2016, from https://kinginstitute.stanford.edu/king-papers/documents/loving-your-enemies

King, M. L. (1963, August 28). "King Speaks to March on Washington." Retrieved from https://kinginstitute.stanford.edu/king-papers/documents/i-have-dream-address-delivered-march-washington-jobs-and-freedom

King, M. L. (1963, April 16). "Letter from Birmingham Jail." Retrieved from https://kinginstitute.stanford.edu/king-papers/documents/letter-birmingham-jail

King, M. L. (1964, December 10). Speech from Nobel Lecture. Retrieved from https://www.nobelprize.org/nobel_prizes/peace/laureates/1964/king-acceptance_en.html

King, M. L. (1965, February 26). Sermon at Temple Israel of Hollywood. Retrieved from http://www.americanrhetoric.com/speeches/mlktempleisraelhollywood.htm

King, M. L. (1967, April 4). "Beyond Vietnam—A Time to Break Silence." Retrieved from http://www.americanrhetoric.com/speeches/mlkatimetobreaksilence.htm

King, M. L. (1968, April 3). I've Been to the Mountaintop. Retrieved from http://www.americanrhetoric.com/speeches/mlkivebeentothemountaintop.htm

King, M. L. (1968). Stanford: The King Institute Resources. Martin Luther King, Jr. and the Freedom Global Struggle. "I've Been to the Mountaintop." Retrieved from http://kingencyclopedia.stanford.edu/encyclopedia/documentsentry/ive_been_to_the_mountaintop/

King, M. L. (2008, April 3). "Remembering MLK's Prophetic 'Mountaintop' Speech." NPR Radio *(Morning Edition)*. Retrieved from http://www.npr.org/templates/story/story.php?storyId=89326670

King, M. L. (2012, November 16). "MLK Quote of the Week: Sticking to Love" (blog post). Retrieved from http://www.thekingcenter.org/blog/mlk-quote-week-sticking-love

King, M. L. (2015, June 20). "Martin After Elijah: 'America May Go to Hell.'" Retrieved from http://noirg.org/articles/martin-after-elijah-america-may-go-to-hell/

Kytle, E. J., and B. Roberts. (2015, March 14). "Birth of a Freedom Anthem." *The New York Times*. Retrieved from https://www.nytimes.com/2015/03/15/opinion/sunday/birth-of-a-freedom-anthem.html?_r=0

Marsh, C. (2013, January 17). "Where Do We Go From Here? Remembering the Life and Trials of Martin Luther King, Jr." *Religion & Politics*, p.1. Retrieved from http://religionandpolitics.org /2013/01/17/where-do-we-go-from-here-remembering-the-life-and-trials-of-martin-luther-king-jr/

Nguyen, V. (2017, January 16). "15 of Martin Luther King Jr.'s Most Inspiring Motivational Quotes." *Parade*. Retrieved from https://parade.com/252644/viannguyen/15-of-martin-luther-king-jr-s-most-inspiring-motivational-quotes/

Younge, G. (2013, August 9). "Martin Luther King: The Story Behind His 'I Have a Dream' Speech." *The Guardian*. Retrieved from https://www.theguardian.com/world/2013/aug/09/martin-luther-king-dream-speech-history

ACKNOWLEDGMENTS

To research this book, I consulted many sources, including books and videos. The most compelling research, however, came from the men and women who witnessed the events surrounding Martin Luther King, Jr.'s death, either from their firsthand experience or through television accounts, radio broadcasts, or newspaper articles from the time of his tragic death. I wish to thank Ambassador Andrew Young for imparting his memories.

Special thanks to the following people and institutions: Smithsonian Institute's National Museum of African American Heritage and Culture, the Schomburg Center for Research in Black Culture, and especially to Samuel R. Rubin, education specialist at the John F. Kennedy Presidential Library and Museum. Gratitude goes to Natalia Remis and Jewel Benton for their research assistance. I gratefully acknowledge Ron Roth for his preliminary fact checking of the manuscript and the time line from 1929–1967. And to David Lovett for his extraordinary and generous consultation and meticulous fact checking of the "Now Is the Time" photo history on pages 118–121, the 1968 portion of the time line, as well as the interior text. We are also grateful for the help and continued support from Karen Van Rossem and Deimosa Webber-Bey from the Scholastic Library, and from Amla Sanghvi of Scholastic's photo research department.

I wish to thank Janine Antoni and her husband, Paul Ramirez, whose gathering of friends on the eve of Martin Luther King, Jr.'s birthday helped inspire this book's creation.

To Dianne Hess, an editor of superior spiritual insight, thank you for your skilled embrace of this book's concept and scope. Art director Marijka Kostiw, your creative vision is unparalleled.

This book's soul was illuminated by the civil rights recollections of my late father, Philip J. Davis, and my mother, Gwendolyn Snow Davis, to whom I offer continued gratitude for giving me a firm foundation to my heritage. Finally, thank you to my husband, Brian Pinkney. You inspire me every day.

The text in this book was set in 14pt. Adobe Garamond Pro.
Garamond is a group of many old-style serif typefaces, originally designed by Parisian
craftsman Claude Garamond and other sixteenth century French engravers.
There are now many modern revivals.

The display font is Perpetua Titling MT Light.
Perpetua is a serif typeface that was designed by English sculptor and stonemason Eric Gill
for the British Monotype Corporation. Perpetua is named for the Christian martyr
Vibia Perpetua, whose text was used in one of its first showings.

Brian Pinkney created his paintings with watercolor, gouache, and India ink on watercolor paper.
The book was edited by Dianne Hess.
It was art directed and designed by Marijka Kostiw.
Manufacturing was supervised by Shannon Rice.

This book was printed and bound by R. R. Donnelley in China.